AF614046

Love Stands

by
Lacey

authorHOUSE®

AuthorHouse™
1663 Liberty Drive
Bloomington, IN 47403
www.authorhouse.com
Phone: 1 (800) 839-8640

Published by AuthorHouse 08/23/2019

ISBN: 978-1-4490-8135-5 (sc)
ISBN: 978-1-4490-8136-2 (hc)

Library of Congress Control Number: 2010901105

Print information available on the last page.

Dedication

I thank my mother Betty Frances Groves for music and song. She always pushed me to sing in church. She taught me about Jesus and for that I am so thankful. Precious is a mother who loves the Lord and teaches their children to fear God.

I thank my dad that even though his tough love came 10.00 dollars a dozen for me. I thank him for pushing me and my sister Kim, to sing together. We were on the radio as little girls. Hoping! One day to make it, to Nashville Tennessee. My father is a great guitarist, violin, mandolin, and a banjo player.

Love Stands

This is a real life love *story* about a woman who fell in love to a man with a name same as her last name. They meet under very different circumstances. They meet after Lacey's sister goes to the North Woods and opens up her own Barbershop. In an old town when Wisconsin first became a state back in 1857 called Rhinelander Wisconsin, town of the Hodag's. Lacey's sister opens up a Barbershop and meets a man called Adam Wenk. She talked to him after continually cutting his hair for two years. She asked questions on top of questions hoping maybe this guy was for her sister Lacey. After almost three years her sister *calls* Lacey and tells her about Adam Wenk. *At* this time Lacey is alone, but skeptical about this man never having girl friends. He just stayed home with his parents for thirty-five years. Lacey at this time is in Florida helping her little brothers and sister. Her mother's health is better, but she has episodes of asthma and headaches. Lacey is twenty-three and meets the wrong man. Have two children a son first named Charles and a daughter named Tabetha. A tragic accident happens to her daughter. She becomes crippled and diagnosed with cerebral palsy. Lacey never married the children's father. Later he gets killed in a gunfight and Lacey is left to raise the children on her own. Earlier when Lacey was sixteen she had high hopes on meeting the husband of her dreams. The wedding dress she bought in New Jersey is seventy-five years old. An antique she kept to wear for the true love of her life. She often goes to her chest that Mrs. Nicolas her Aunt in the Carolinas gave her, before she past along with old, secret recipes that one day Lacey hopes to have her own jams and jellies for sale. That's one thing Lacey always admired Mrs. Nicolas. Lacey calls her mama Nicolas. She had her own home made wines that she sold to help cure pain. She was a great woman and still lives on today in Lacey.

All Along the two years Lacey; is in Florida fighting her own battles with a man that stepped in to her life unexpectedly. She is struggling has two children Tabetha and Charles. She is not married and always had hopes of meeting the true love of her life. She bought a wedding dress at nineteen years old at an auction in New Jersey for $25.00 dollars. Which was a 1740's wedding dress? It was all lace and had a crown with real baby pearls and a beautiful lace parcels. She put this in a cedar chest and *wherever* she moved, she didn't fail to take the wedding dress with her.

Lacey was determined to meet her true love threw bad weather, storms and rain she was determined. She said her prayers, wished up on those stars and kept the faith. Thou a man that didn't marry her struggling, having two children after he died in a gun fight. She was still determined to wear that wedding dress and meet the man of her dreams. No matter what!

Not knowing her sister was match making after she heard her sister had two children and one winding up with a disability. Lacey's little girl had a tragic accident that left her with cerebral palsy. At the hands of her biological father that left her on the wagon train, while he went into a bar to play cards and drink. Lacey still tried to make the relationship work, but fate had a different plan for her life. Her sister met a man that was perfect for her. Not only the names were the same their mothers were born the same year and their Fathers were born the same year too.

This Story is a true-life story about two people that meet up with each other, fell in love and is still together to this day. Let me tell the story, because I know your all anxious to hear this true story of the year of 2000 it is just dated back in 1857 to make you see the struggle that these two people had finding each other. Another time will tell the story in the year of 2000. This just makes it more interesting being told in this time.

I dedicate this book to my friend Adam Wenk and children, because they mean the world to me. I also thank our father in heaven for not taking me home yet. In 1994 I was in a car accident that left me with a broken jaw, collapsed lung, paralyzed from my waist down, blind, bleeding eternally, broken collar bone fractured spleen and a blood clot in my heart also a Traumatic brain injury. I had died three times and the doctors brought me back. God gave me a second chance at my life. Now I will tell this story how I found true love. I won't forget my brothers Jeff, Tom, and my sisters Penny, Kim, the sister that introduced my husband to me, my little sister Mary that has given me so much hope in love. My step fathers Harry Near that had faith in me.He went to Berlin auction and found three pearls in one oyster and he made me a graduation present, which is a necklace that I treasure, because I feel God put that special oyster there for me. My mother, Betty Francis Groves, my Uncle Marvin and Aunt Clare, for telling me when you set your mind to it you can do anything. You can accomplish anything. My Uncle Marvin and Aunt Clare made me believe in myself and I will love them forever. They deserve the best in life, because they are my angels that helped me recapture myself after my tragic accident. My best friend, Connie Lynn Maizer, Who is my confidant? She helped me see my gifts and told me that God loves me. I also thank my Dad for music and song. My singing talent makes me feel loved. I thank my Brother McDonald for being a father to me when I felt like I didn't have one his love devotion and prayers to God for me kept me from falling away from the cross. My second mom Vera McDonald told me never gives up and don't stop serving God. I love her more than anything in this world for helping me who I am in Christ. Pastor Atkins and his wife that showed my children love and prayed that one-day I would find a father *for* my children. Sister Lindsey who helped me from the African *American* Family that *gave me a* place to stay and food to eat. As a young girl Martin Luther King inspired my life and gave me determination never to give up. God bless many hundreds of other people around the whole world Black, white Chinese, Italian, Greek, an*d many* others that know I am not prejudice that all blood that runs through all of our veins is red. We serve the same God that created the whole world and all people in it. May God bless my family, and enrich them every day that there is a God.

All The names in this story are changed so no one knows

who they are and I have no lawsuits. This story is a real life story that is from the Author Lacey. I hope everyone in this world can learn from this true love story. Call me a hopeless romantic, because I am. Call me a woman of faith; because faith can't be seen it is deep within one's self and if you put it into action after you know it will come true, it becomes a seed that can grow up to be a big tree. In the end it can give you anything you hope for. I hope all are inspired.

This is my first poem I wrote after my car accident.

THE GREAT PAINTER

I look at myself through a glass, which has many colors like a glass at a cathedral. I can call myself a rainbow, in hope one day I find my treasure at the end of this wonderful personality of colors. Do we all know what we are in Jesus? I believe God has a big paintbrush that brushes these true colors into my world. As I walk closer to him. He feels my voids and paints a pretty color in the place of it. As I press forward and at times I slip more colors are painted darker so I can see my mistakes more clearly. The colors that he uses are astonishing to my personality. I glow with a sunlight this world can't comprehend. This is because they don't know him-until you know becomes his painting, you will never be able to fulfill who you are in Jesus. This great painter having made heaven and earth painted all things. His spirit does all things. I have found my treasure. It is behind that great paint brush.

Chapter One

The growing years by Lacey

I am finally nine years old and I get my first horse. I live in South Jersey, on a farm way back in the woods .where there are streams and lots of blue berry bushes. My mother Betsy Fran was born in Summersville West Virginia. She is very sick all the time. My two younger brothers and younger sister depend on me a lot. I cook, clean and do cloths every day. The year is 1836. It is very rough growing up with only going to the store once a month. Other times your gathering eggs and milking cows. What a life of work I live!

I wish things were easier at this time in my life, because I love to just ride my horse Beauty. It is a pretty paint with white and brown spots. She protects me everywhere I go she wants to go. I have such great dreams when I look up at the stars at night. I always pick a different star to wish and pray upon. I also dream about having a great man one day. Getting married and having a son and a daughter. The son would have to be first to take care of the little girl. I want them to have blonde hair, like the sun blue eyes like the sky, and a smile that has two dimples on each side.

Mom is at the doctors and I am patiently waiting for her to return by making an apple pie. I went to the apple groves in Greenwich New Jersey. This is one of the biggest apple groves in South Jersey along with the best cider ever. Were not suppose to sample certain buckets, but I do. That is the stuff that grandfather says that knocks your socks off.

My grandfather Groves is a great man, because he always helps with money and protects his grandchildren. This is my mother's father. He lives with us now, because his wife died and he shouldn't be alone. I am still waiting for my mom and the pie is done. I put it in the window to cool and I drank too much of my dad's cider. I am a little swimmy headed.

Finally mom and dad came home and I felt like a ton of bricks. I guess this is what mom says being soused was. My mother told me what the doctor said. That we would have to move to warm weather or she would die soon.

Your father and I have decided to keep the house and allow your two older sisters to live in the house and take care of it. Your grandfather will stay with them and make sure their o.k. You Mary, Joe and Jake will move to Florida with me and your father. The house in Florida is a big ranch house. I asked when we were leaving because I have a great friend Connie that I love so much. We have been friends since Sunday school years, all of our twelve years of life. We even were baptized together and we asked God to forgive us for our sins. We even had boy thoughts that we shouldn't of and asked a priest together if we were going to go to hell. He hailed Mary, put holy water on our heads and he said we were forgiven. We know all of each other's secrets. I will really miss my best friend.

I ran as fast as I could to tell her that I was leaving, but when I arrived at her house she wasn't there. On the way home all I could think about was her always helping me with my math. She is very smart and all the kids make fun of her. I think to myself who will stop them from picking on her. I always stood up to them and when I am around they don't say a word after I smacked Lisa for throwing sand in Connie's eyes.

I made it home and mom had some pie and told me they will take as much stuff as they can and come back in a month for the rest. This is a new experience for us children, because we have never been to Florida. John is younger than Jake, he is nine and Jake is eleven. Mary is six years old at this time and everyone is growing up so fast. Skeet which is sixteen and Caroline which is eighteen will be living together in our home in Jersey. Caroline is married and has two children Lindsey and Robbie. Her husband is named Robert he is a military man and is stationed all over.

Skeet told mom and dad she is moving to Rhinelander Wisconsin and is going to open up a barber shop. She works really hard cutting people's hair. Its moving day tomorrow, but before we go we will go to church for the last time. I can't wait to see Mr. Phillips, because he is a Great pastor. We all had church and said our goodbye's and we all cried. I finally said goodbye to Connie and we promised when we grow up will find each other again.

Well the sun is up and my faithful bane rooster is crowing at 4:00 o: clock in the morning. I raise Bane chickens and sale my eggs in town to make my own money. My faithful chickens will come with me to start a new life. Along with My potbelly pig called Dandy, we call him Dandy, because she was found in a Dandelion field. My wolf and a domestic cat called shadow. We took our horse, cows and a few goats.

Jason my father said we couldn't fit anything else so let's get in the wagon and go. We went through town and they had a sign saying they will miss our family. We started singing amazing grace and they all came out and waved.

I didn't know why my mom didn't get her healing, but it didn't shake me none maybe her healing is up ahead.

As the heat was very hot and exhausting the sweat poured down my face like cups of water. I felt my heart racing and I keep putting my mother's face with a wet soft cloth. Hoping she would be cooled off. It was hot for me, but more exhausting for mom, because of her sickness. I just hope and pray she will make this long trip to Florida. In my mind I feel everything happens for a reason, but something's can be redirected in your life to bring a positive energy flow to your future. My grandfather always said life is like a garden. Plant good seeds of faith and hope and love to your fellow man". Your garden of life will bring a good crop, which is your future. Bad seeds are things you do to harm other people, because of your own misfortunes. Maybe if you just were thankful with what the creator gave you then when you won't have a bad crop.

I really miss my grandfather: his words of wisdom are great encouragement today. I often feel that my older peers are my angels here on earth guiding me. Even after they go to heaven their voices still speak to me. I know they all must be looking down at me. I am a very protective person over the older people. The Cherokee

Chief in North Carolina named me Baby Bear. I often

wonder why he named me that. Maybe, because I am short. All of these pictures running through my mind making me feel bad that I had to leave my best friend, Lynn we grew up together one year apart. We always wanted to have a double wedding and married brothers. Then maybe we could raise our children together. I am only nine so we have time to see each other again. Sometimes it's better to leave friendships and then in the future connect again. It makes you appreciate of your friendship. My mother Betty Fran says, "Distance always makes the heart grow fonder".

Well the atmosphere feels much lighter and pressure *seems* like it is getting less. Dawn is setting in and we traveled for about 200 miles across the mountains. I feel real hungry and very tired, because I am worried about my mother. My dad finally stops to camp for the night where the most prettily waterfalls you ever could see. It is spring and the mountains are so pretty. I get off the wagon train and right away I see wild strawberries, black berries, raspberries, and a wild plumb tree. I help my mom off of the wagon and put her on a blanket. Night will be soon, so I started working fast. I collected firewood and picked all different kinds of berries and plumbs. I made plum sauce and mixed berry pie. I fried my two hens after my dad butchers them. I made Indian bread and brought along three pounds of homemade sweet butter. My family ate so much they all fell asleep, under the most beautiful full moon lit sky with silver bright stars. Oh! How secure I feel with my mom, dad, little brothers and little sister. This is why I like to live for my family to be taken care of They are very comforted by me and me by them.

Looking at the stars, wondering if my future husband is thinking of me tonight. I brought my 1740's wedding dress I bought at an auction before I left New Jersey. It is all lace and white as snow. Hoping that one day I will wear for the man of my dreams. I look around and then fall fast asleep and I dream. I dream about an Indian boy and his tribe. I dreamed of my mother being on a white stallion. I took the dream and put it in my heart believing that one-day my mom would be healed. I say my prayer every day. My faith is Baptist I believe if you believe in Christ, because he died for the whole world. Not just a certain group of people. Go to heaven or a certain church, but all that believe go to *heaven*.

As I hear my bane rooster crow at four in the morning my eyes don't want to open. The sun comes out pretty early. I collect my eggs from my twelve hens. I make toast, eggs, and potatoes for breakfast. I also make fresh coffee and plum sauce poured over apple pie. Breakfast was great and I checked on my mom. She had already been up reading a poetry book. Mom seems to be breathing easier. Her color looks better and she is smiling. We get done eating; I wash the pots, pans and silverware. I load everything up and we're off again through the Appalachian Mountains this time. Where my Aunt Clare and my Uncle Marvin live. They live in Clyde North Carolina. They are my dad's family and my Aunt and Uncle. I love them so much, because they care. They believe in God, too. They have two children, Katherine, she is married to Carl and

Steven, he is not married. He works on their farm and takes care of his parents. He has a loving heart. He likes the color of my blonde hair. We always get along and he helps me pick blackberries in Medford's pasture. I can't wait to see them all. None of them have children at this time, but maybe in the near future. My Aunt Clare grows a nice garden *every* year an*d her* potatoes are so sweet. You can tell she has a lot *of* love to give to her garden. Aunt Clare always said the more you pull the weeds the bigger the potato.

While on the road we see a mountain lion and a wild horse that followed us for a longtime. So dad put a rope around his neck and at first he made loud sounds and jumped. Then I gave him some berries and sugar cubes and he calmed down. By the wounds on his back he seemed like he was beaten. Maybe I'll is able to tame this pretty gray Appaloosa. On the way we saw two skunks mating and a baby bear cub. Dad said to keep our distance, because the mother is around somewhere looking for her cub. Sure enough a little further the mother shows up. We stay our distance and she gets her cub and chases it toward this mountain. Where they probably live. She looked back and by her sound she made it was like a thank you for protecting her baby. This was pretty scary to see, but also making our trip very interesting. I said it would be a very interesting trip.

As we traveled 200 more miles we finally had to stop to spend the night in the Great Smokey Mountains where the people that live here call this "God's Country". The people that live here are different. They keep their word and are very friendly. They have a lot of talent, because they are great musicians. The five-string banjo, fiddle, violin, mandolin, harmonica, and guitar are their entertainment. On Sundays they go to the Baptist church in the valley and sing amazing grace. This valley they call, Maggie Valley. The minister talks about loving thy neighbor, the greatest gift of all.

As we start to find a place to camp a little elderly lady and man came by and asked if we would like some good home cooking and a place to sleep inside tonight. They said it would be our pleasure to give.

You all have good hospitality. We said ok and traveled two miles to their home. It was a ranch of 40 horses, chickens, cattle, and pigs. My goodness they were so happy to have us over. What a night to remember. We did not go to bed till I2:00 midnights. What a night to remember. We showed up at their house and glory and behold. The nicest looking boy I ever did see. It was her son she had when she went through the change of life. She had two little girls that got along with my brothers. So we all sat down to eat and her son Josh couldn't keep his eyes off of me. It made me feel nice and warm to have the attention. I just want to wait for Mr. Right. So we all danced except mom and my dad they watched us kids. They played the fiddle and the five-string banjo. Josh was great on the five strings and his dad played the fiddle real good. He even danced while playing it.

Then mom and dad went to bed in Josh's room and us kids slept in sleeping bags on the floor. The fire was burning and the house was so peaceful. I actually regretted going back on the road. It makes me appreciate what I really have when I am away from home. Well I wake up to three roosters crowing this morning and the sound of bacon frying along with pancakes and eggs. I ask if I can help and she said you're a guest. Just maybe you could go outside and get the bucket of milk. As I went to get the milk a little prairie dog jumped out and ran. Somehow he had gotten the cover off and helped himself to some milk. The adventure still goes on.

Through the Great Smokey Mountains

How God made these mountains so beautiful. They call this Gods country that makes me think it's just like heaven. How" God made this Gods country. The mountains are just breath taking. The mountains are Smokey looking in the morning. The birds are singing and the flowers are in full bloom. I ask dad to stop so I can take a rest in the woods. I went in the woods to relieve myself and glory and behold I seen the most beautiful Indian tribe I have ever seen. The women *were* as *pretty* as the sunset in the evening. The men looked like warriors and were tall with black raven hair and a look of strength. These were the Cherokee Indians. They have come a long way from the trail of tears. They looked at me and raised their hands in peace. I didn't want to alarm anyone so I kept it a secret. I believe they knew that my mother's health was bad. A man called the spirit man threw dust at me from a pouch. This was the day that the spirit worked in our lives. Mom even ate after we traveled 200 more miles. We slept in the woods this time and built a fire. Mom could not get enough chicken. This showed me that mom would eventually get her healing.

We went to sleep and I had a dream of an Indian boy that came into my life to protect me. I also dreamed that mom was finally healed by a medicine man from a Semenov tribe in Florida. I awoke and told my mom my dream. She said it was a dream of hope that was reassuring me everything would be all right.

We ate breakfast and started off again on our adventure. We only have to travel 100 miles to my Aunt Clare and Uncle Marvin's house. I can't wait to get there and see my cousin Steve. He was always a nice person and cared very much for everyone. I always admired him when he sang and treated us like his brothers and sisters. I remember a few years back picking blackberries in med- fords pasture. They were so big and sweet, that my Aunt Clare always made black bevy cobbler. It was great, because she had an old milk cow that really put out great milk. With black berry cobbler and a glass of milk fresh from the cow was great. The cow's name was Sally Lee. She was a nice cow, but I still remember getting my stomach poked by her. I remember Booger their little dog that loved to play around with bears. Uncle Marvin always said he could tree anything, it was his prize dog.

I ponder on all of these things like camping out on Warf Pin. A mountain our bloodline has owned for centuries.

It was called Warf Pin because all of the cattle were raised there and put threw big wharfs to ship off the mountain and take to market. What a great place it is, because the last time I was there I caught 19 fish for breakfast to feed the whole family. It's a silent place except for nature and the listening to the Cherokee drums that played at night on Devils Court House where the Cherokee Indians drove evil spirits from the Appalachian Mountains. I could hear a mysterious sound and knew the drums were doing something good in the spirit world. Sometimes on that mountain I heard them all night long. Then in the morning the birds would sound a peaceful nature sound of peace. I still believe the drums are to fight for peace.

I still hear the cries of the spirits of the Cherokee people that died on the Trail of Tears. My bloodline came from that long trail of tears. It has made me very strong to be part of the Cherokee *people. I feel acceptance even* thou I am *part* white. Inside I am *a Cherokee* even thou I have platinum gold hair. It is something when your mixed you always have to prove yourself, but there is something about me I never had to prove myself to them. They could feel I was their sister. We go to the POW wow and watch the chief dance war dances and dances of peace. He is so beautiful with lots of pretty colored feathers that he looks like a colored eagle. I call them spirit men, because some of the spirit men heal. For some reason they wear a lot of different birds feet around their neck. I can't wait to get there and see them.

We're almost there and I am so tired of traveling, but my mom is breathing a lot easier. She even looks real happy and bright today. She *doesn't* say much, but I know my mother is strong and won't give up. She has great faith in the creator above. Were about fifty miles away and should make it before dark. None of us say anything and just watch all kinds of animals. We saw a female bear that lost her cubs that we found. Thank God none of us got close to the cubs the mother bear will try to scare you away. We saw a skunk, porky pine, eagles flying over head and two Eagles fighting over a fish. I want to see a parakeet and keep it as a pet. They say they are so pretty in Florida. It has been exciting traveling through these mountains so far. My two little brothers and little sister are sleeping and I just keep rambling on in my head about all of the beauty I see. Like the sunsets, double rainbow's and pretty crystal skies at night sleeping under the stars. I started to write a poem in my mind. Here is the poem.

THE MORNING SUN

Oh! Morning sun as I awake in the morning. With a smile on my face. Precious is your beauty. To know your radiance exists, it is great to the world. For no one can look at the sun and not smile. When I get up, the sun refreshes the world. In the morning it is so peaceful over the ocean. It brings things to life. Without this life would not exist. Without God's son I would not exist. For his son is brighter than the world's sun.

I write a lot of poems and hope that I will have poetry book one day. Along with a nice husband, a son and daughter. I hope to have a nice wedding in the mountains one-day. Life is so nice in the Carolinas. I hope to have a place in these mountains one day just to come in the spring. The flowers and the smell of spring are just like walking into heaven. It gives off serenity.

Well were almost to the Cherokee tribe and I look around and see the trees how *they* look so special, because the Indians are very spiritual people and they bless their land. I hear the drums beating were almost around the corner and my brothers are anxious to meet their friends.

My mom looks a lot better and she is finishing the blanket for white feather. I have a couple of things for my friend too. I have a doll that I brought. It has black hair and it's dressed in white. My dad has a knife for his friend the chief. My brothers have two fishing poles to show their two friends how white people fish.

We are finally there *and I* see ten Indians in the trees up on the ridge waiting for us. They are all dressed in their feathers and headdress. *They* are beautiful to look at all dressed up. Especially this one Indian that has red, blue, and yellow feathers he looks a little unsure of us. I hope he will eventually loosen up and be friendly. I am one that hates hurt feelings and fighting. Then all of a sudden they all gather around my family and me. They all say welcome, but the one Indian unsure touched my hand and smiled. I was happy that he was kind, because I sure was sort of unsure of him, at first. He seemed very dominant.

We go in and lots of fires are burning and the smell of buffalo stew and venison was in the air. I love to eat there cooking, because the Indian women cook to please the whole tribe and not just their selves. The Indian women reach up to the wagon to help my mother off and embrace her. My mother looked so happy she had tears in her *eyes,* she loved the affection. She seen her friend that she didn't see for four years, they hugged each other. My friend came out and she had grew tall. She is a little taller than I am. She still dresses in white buckskin and white feathers in her hair. She is still very special to her tribe. *My* two brothers jump off the wagon with their fishing poles and found their friends and started playing right away to the mountaintop where they always fished *an*d swam. Eagle feather and little bear *foot w*ere their two friend's names. *My* dad didn't get off the wagon until the chief came to him. He said! My old friend come and sits by the fire! It helps my legs that are getting older. My father replied! I guess we're all getting older! My dear friend, I have a gift for you. The chief said! I have a gift for you to. My father gave him a leather package and in it was the prettiest buckskin knife with the prettiest eagle on the handle. The chief was pleased. Then he gave my father a pretty shirt that his wife made with the prettiest bear on the back. Then they went into the tent and smoked the peace pipe. Four other Indians followed into the Tepee.

We all played with our friends while the grownups prepared for the POW Wow. It was fine because white feather and me went horseback riding up to where my brothers were and teased them.

Calling them all cowards. They ran after us and *they* couldn't catch us because they didn't have horses, but it was fun because the Indian boys could run almost as fast as the horse. Finally we went black berry picking and had enough to make a pie. They make their pies by frying them. White feathers mother white dove made them while we sat and ate venison jerky. The boys came down off the mountain and started eating and talking to us. One especially that tried to catch me on the horse kept asking me if I had a man. I said no and I am too young. White feather laughed, because when they get thirteen they start preparing the males and females. It is different in the white world, because of our customs. I would rather be in their world it is not as complicated. Well the drums are starting to play and we all are around the bomb fire. The men start to dance and the women all line up. Jr. is a custom to honor the men by standing when they dance. *They are* really getting into dancing. I am so glad that it is finally getting started. The Indian boy called little bear foot is dressed so pretty he looks like a raven in flight. He turns around and around and spreads his wings oh how pretty it is to watch the men dance. Then the men stop and the women take their places and start a two step dance. They are so pretty all dressed up in pretty soft colors. It is so sacred and the Indian men stay real still and quiet, because they respect their women.

Then they stop and we all start to make plates of food. My mother brought her best china for this occasion.

After everyone made his or her plates the chief spoke a prayer for us all and it went like this. Great Spirit thanks you for your presence and for your great earth of food for us. Thank you for our friends that have *come* to share in the abundances of your creation. Bless the tribe and my friends. May our spirits embrace each other forever? My mom started to be teary eyed, but then stopped, because she felt so happy. Then we all started to eat and the chief got his wild berry punch out and boy it was good. Then we all danced together around the fire until about 12; 00 midnight. Then we all went to sleep. We woke up the next morning and traveled back to Aunt Clare and Uncle Marvin's place. We s*ti*ll have five more days there.

Before we left they gave us each an arrowhead meaning good luck. They all waved goodbye in Indian and mom started to cry like always. I can't wait to get back and see if I can find more crawl dads. I also want to pick some black berries and raspberries. My brothers wished they could stay on the reservation forever. They both have Indian headpieces on from their friends. They went fishing while they were there and caught actually 25 trout and gave them to their friend. The Indian boys told the chief they caught them, but the chief shook his head *like* where is the spear whole. They couldn't explain it well as we travel back to my Aunts I am sure a great adventure it will be.

This is what I write on the way back to my Aunt and Uncles house.

Life Has No promises

> One day it's raining and one day it snows one day it's cloudy an*d* one day the wind blows. Everything is so unpredictable in this world in which we live, but we all know from the day we are born, time is running out. From one day to the next we do not know what the future holds. But for sure whoever is born, they must one-day die. Life is just like the wind. You never know when it is going to blow. Everything has its season a season to bloom, a season to fall, a season to grow and a season to die. God made everything in rhythm with his nature. That's why life has no promises and we cannot predict tomorrow, for we do not know if tomorrow will come.

This is a memorial to four teenagers that 1 comforted in

the year of 2000 outside my house in Wisconsin that died. I loved them very much and wished I could have saved their lives after a tragic car accident. Robin, Corey, Richard and Adam are loved and remembered forever.

This also became a memorial song for nine eleven tragedy on a memorial disc by Magic Key Productions Hollywood California.

After writing this poem I realize there are no promises in life. You never know when you're going to die. I often think of losing my mother to this sickness that she has. I hope we can find her healing. I believe the great creator has healing for everyone in this world. You just have to find it. Sometimes it comes in the most mysterious ways. As we keep traveling and we see a little lady that is waving on the side of the street. She claims that her horse got away and she needs help, because her wagon train went over the bank with all her belongings. So we helped her get all her belongings up to the road. We told her we couldn't stay, but when we *get to* our Aunts we would finally send help. We have a sick *person* that needs to get to Florida as quick as possible.

So she understood our reasons and waved goodbye. Her name was Mrs. Annie Thompson that liked the moonshine. They say she would help Mr. Lacey deliver the shine through the mountains to a lot of tribal people in Cherokee North Carolina. It was made in Rhinelander and Edgar areas in Wisconsin. Shortly we were over the next mountain and glory and behold there was Aunt Claries and Uncle Marvin's place. We went up their steep driveway and the happiest two people on the porch smiling and saying welcome. Oh! How those nice words that I heard made me so happy. They were my favorite aunt and uncle. They are always warm in their hearts toward all people. They never judge and they always have good to say about everyone.

We get off the wagon and the first thing I smell is bisque's, gravy and sausage, all ready for us to eat. So I hug my Aunt Clare and Uncle Marvin and tell them I love and miss them. Aunt Clare takes us in the house and sits us down to the table to eat. We will spend five days here with them. I eat and eat and eat some more, than I go out to the creek and drink their ice cold spring water. I seen two crawl dads that were so cute, but one clipped my finger and it hurt. I seen a garden snake so I picked it up and put it in Aunt Clare's garden to eat bugs. Then their dog booger kept jumping up and down wanting me to throw a stick for him to catch. I played with booger for a while and then went to sleep in the daisy field in Medford's pasture. I dreamed of the tribal people being very *close* to my mother and me.

I dreamed that she cooked food *for* them. I dreamed that a medicine man healed my mother. I remember dancing around a fire while the drums played. I dreamed I went to Florida and made an Indian friend whose name is Lone star. His father's name was keeper of the fire.

I then hear a soft voice say it's time to come in and eat dinner. It was my Uncle Marvin; he always knew where my secret places were. He always looked after me, because I was always the smallest. I was named from the Cherokee tribe in North Carolina when I was just four. They called me Baby Bear, because I am small, but very strong. I have a very bad temper when I am upset. So I wake up and go to the house with my Uncle Marvin.

He said he missed me and that I am getting bigger. It makes me happy when he complements me. My father does not do that. So I don't get any encouragement except for when I go to North Carolina to see Aunt Clare and Uncle Marvin. My mother gives me encouragement, but she is sick and I try to always encourage her. I know she loves me very much even thou I do not get a lot of encouragement from her. I am sure she is worried about her sickness.

I am at the table with my family and Aunt Clare made *the* best friend chicken dumplings and potatoes and beans fresh from her garden. It is so good. Then we all listen to my dad play the five strings and Aunt Clare plays the guitar. We kids were too full to dance. Then we hear the drums from the Cherokee Indian reservation.

I love the sound of the drums beating on the Indian reservation. We will go their tomorrow to trade with them. I have a girl friend on the reservation that I play with. We play hiding go seek and we chase each other and play tag. I can't wait to see white feather. She has white feathers in her hair. Well it's time to go to sleep *and* we all ford our places and we all go to sleep. I say my prayer-Creator of all things I pray for my whole family and the healing of my Mother-Amen.

I wake up to the rooster crowing, the smell of eggs and bacon frying. I hope my Aunt Clare made her butter milk biscuits, because maybe I can take white feather one, because she loves my Aunt Clare's biscuits. I hear Aunt Clare singing to try to get everyone up. So I hurry and get dressed and go down to the creek to catch some crawl dads. White Feather and I like to play with them. I caught five crawl dads and some stick bates. It is these little worms in a cocoon that we fish with. I found two dozen so I can teach white feather to fish with a hook. They spear their fish and it takes skill that I don't have. I always want to contribute to the large diner that the Indians prepare for my family and me. My grandmother was Cherokee, which died by small pox before I was born. I am very pleased to have been accepted on the reservation even thou I am part white. Where white people wonder about me, because of my white hair the Indian people know I am a part of them.

Well were sitting at the table and eating breakfast. My dad said it would be good to see Chief Sitting Bull again he loved my grandmother and always-told wonderful stories about her on the reservation. I can't wait to leave so I am hurrying to eat my food and put all my stuff in the wagon. Mom says slow down was not going to church this morning. You act like you're going to choke on your food. Will get to the reservation in due time. Aunt Clare asks if we will be back, but my dad said it's hard to tell when those kids get together with the Indian children. They're gone for hours and Betsy Fran loves to sit, talk and sew with White Feathers *mother* Eagle Feather. So if they ask us to spend the night we will. So don't *worry* my *father* say's to Aunt Clare! She always worries that something is going to happen, but she is always write. 1 am glad you can never pull anything over aren't Aunt Clare, because she is always ten steps ahead of everyone else. I believe she has some kind of heavenly gifts. I feel warm when she is around, because she has never hurt my feelings. I can't forget Uncle Marvin, because he is just as gifted as she is.

Well we take off to the Cherokee Indian reservation. Mom and dad said we will go through Maggie Valley where everything is in frill bloom, because it is springtime at its fullest in North Carolina. I know I will see flowers that are bigger than two of my hands. The sight I will see is something out of a dream, (I believe this is God's Country). So we start to go down the road to a place about 40 miles away. Which isn't too far? I start to see field's that are just breath taking, because of the morning sun and the pink yellow and scarlet sky's that had little bit of blue. It seems like that I was just appointed to be there, because the sky's were just painted just for me and my mother, because she kept saying (These skies give me strength) today. Do you ever think that the creation in this world was made for all of us to enjoy? I believe so, because inspiration is what makes us all feel special when we see a rainbow after the rain. The painted sky in Florida after a hard nice rain that sounds like the skies is falling down. So mysterious life is, but so special the creator makes us feel when we just can't find the answers to everyday life. I look at my mother and I wish I could take her pain away, because I love her so much that my heart is broken everyday wondering how much time she has left. I know this 40-mile trip will inspire her and maybe I can find some ginseng to make her some healing tea. Along with some bloodroot to put on her cracked hands. Her hands are dry and have sores on them from the cold winters. These mountains are healing even the spring water replenishes your health and makes you feel so good inside to have a nice glass of water from running off these great mountains. As we travel closer and closer to our destiny I see the trail of tears where my ancestors the Cherokee Indians traveled to the Appalachian Mountains. Spring is so beautiful that I feel I have gone to heaven smelling of the rodeadenrin and the lilacs as big as watermelons. The mountain fragrance is so breath taking to smell. As we travel we see the water running off of the mountains from deep within the rocks. I cannot wait to see the Great waterfall called sliding rock. We will camp there tonight and then I can go hunting for the ginseng and bloodroot for my mother. We are almost there, but as we get closer there is more wild life. A mountain lion and a lot of Cardinals, and an eagle showing, her young how to fly! So much nature to see and ponder on, because nature to me is what life is all about. Watching nature makes me appreciate Gods creation and makes me feel even more loved to know a higher power is watching out for me. At times in life, I know I have to ponder on God's creation, knowing that I am loved to make it through the Great hardships up ahead for me. Challenges are to be challenged back at the challenge that has been given to you. I feel everything happens for a reason, but along with this you can use wisdom in all you do. I feel you can also prevent things from happening that are evil. Enough of my deep thought's! Life is looking like paradise. My birthday is June 28, 1848 my birthday is tomorrow. This is a great birthday present, because I enjoy the mountains I feel loved by Gods Country. I always loved to come to North Carolina and be with my Aunt Clare and Uncle Marvin. My two favorite people in the world, I always felt loved and wanted to be the apple of their eye. I felt this was my home and my way of life. I regret not growing up here around good down to earth southern people. I met a few people that were very kind along the way as people passed in their wagons and buggies. They waved and asked *how* we were doing. We are almost there, I hear the waterfall. I hope a camping spot will be right by the waterfall, because the waterfall puts me to sleep at night. We go around the corner and see the prettiest red roses I have ever seen in my life. That was my present for flowers on my birthday. I always loved picking flowers for myself on my birthday. In *hopes Twill* have a man *to* bring *me* flowers one day? For now, I will enjoy being a little girl and in *my* own world of dreams. I then look up and see the waterfall. It has a rainbow in it that is so beautified I color it is all soft colors. It seemed so powerful with its radiant light. That I could wish for anything and it would appear.

This is what I write in a thought of innocence.

> Pretty it is to see this beauty from the top of this cliff. I see for miles the beauty of the Appalachian Mountains. There is no other beauty like this in the spring. Also; in my youth. Then we are on our way down the mountain and on the road we are again.

We travel and finally after a few hours were back at Aunt Clare's again. She had diner on and a pot of coffee along with fried bread. We sat and talked about our adventure and she wanted to know all about it. We all talked for hours. Finally we had diner and went to bed. Before we went to bed we told Aunt Clare we were leaving in the morning. Tears were in her eyes and she said make sure you come back real soon. I love Aunt Clare and Uncle Marvin they are my favorite. They understand me where no one else does at times. I feel excepted by them.

I get up to the sound of bacon frying and eggs. Aunt Clare is cooking a fare well breakfast. We all get up eat and didn't say much, because we hate when Aunt Clare cries. So we ate and finally said we have to be on our way. We said our goodbyes after packing and down the road we went. Watching Aunt Clare cry. Uncle Marvin comforted her by hugging her. He is such a good man I hope I am lucky enough to meet someone like him one day for my husband.

We traveled for hours then set up camp. We repeated this for four days and then finally made it to Florida. It started to get real hot so I put on a pair of knee high shorts and a summer top. We saw the ocean and dad let us go swimming for a bit. We had so much fun riding the waves. I said were finally here and I love it. My little brothers loved it to.

Finally we are back in the wagon and four hours away. We should make it by nightfall dad said. What an adventure it has been since we reached Florida. We keep moving on and dad said there are wild Indians, gunslingers, and wild horses. It sounds sort of scary, but I am always ready for a great adventure.

We travel to our home, and what a sight to see beaches, sunshine and palm trees. This seemed like heaven to me. I start to see our land and the six bed room house. It is like a big colonial home. There is a big barn that houses about twenty horses. We have orange, lemon and lime trees.

We arrive and get out of the wagon. Mother is very tired, so I then make her bed and she fell fast asleep. As my dad, Joe and John put the wagon and horses away; I cleaned the house and put a big ham in the oven. I made string beans, mashed potatoes and corn bread. For desert I made a German apple cake like mom makes.

I went out on the porch and seen a bald eagle fly over the property. I always felt they were good luck! It seemed every time I seen one, something wonderful happened. I set the table and called dad, Joe John and Mary to diner. Mom is tired so I will make sure mom eats later. They all came in sat down and told me everything smells good. I replied! I just hope everything tastes good. Dad prayed and said I am sure everything will taste real good Lord. I smiled, because it makes me feel so good when everything is just Wright. I try to be a perfectionist at everything I do. Dad says I'll make someone a good wife someday.

We all ate and talked about moms health. Dad, Joe, and John talked about taking cattle to Jersey. That is the highest price for cattle in the U.S at this time. I heard mom and I went to her, I helped her up and brought her to the table. She said Lacey you made a good diner. I smiled and said thank you mom. She said I can always count on my little girl. It makes me feel good when she calls me her little girl.

Mom ate and ate and then she asked me if I could help her outside on the porch. I went to her right away and helped her. I asked her after she was settled on the porch if she wanted desert? She replied a little later with a cup of tea. I waited with mom on the porch and talked about Jersey and all the things I had to leave behind. Like my best friend Connie. I miss our talks and our times we went swimming black berry picking, blue berry picking and going to church. We sung together in a choir and I sung solo's. Amazing Grace and upon the cross of Calvary was everyone's favorite. Mom just said distance makes the heart grow fonder and you will see her again. Tears came to my eyes, because I have a soft heart. Mom always said when I asked her why I cry sometimes at heartfelt stories. She always said God made me to show the world that angels cry to, because I am one of Gods little angels. That made me cry even more when she said that, because then I know that God loves me and the whole world. I love the whole world to.

Mom sat and had a cup of tea and a piece of German

apple cake then she went to bed along with Joe, John, Mary and dad. I cleaned the dishes and put everything away and sat on the porch with a cup of tea looking up at the full moon and the stars. I then went to the barn and climbed up in the loft. I shined my lantern around and seen a boy sleeping. He had long black hair down his back, with feathers in it. He didn't have a shirt on, but he did have a leather skirt. He had a pretty turquoise necklace on shaped into a half of a moon. He opened his eyes and I asked him his name? He replied I am Lone star! I told him my name is Lacey. We own the property. He asked if it was o.k. to be here and I replied! Yes! I then said I was going to sleep.

As I left the barn and went inside I pondered on Lone star. What a great friend I have found. We connected Wright away it seemed like. Sometimes in life you really can find certain people you can really bond with Wright away. Like my friend Connie in New Jersey. First time we met we wanted to have a pajama party we were only five years old. We grew up to be just like sisters. I wonder what she would think of Lone star.

I finally went to bed and fell fast asleep. I dreamed of a medicine man and his wife. They came to the house and made my mother well. I dreamed the Indian woman danced and took eagle feathers in her hands. She then moved them back and forth over my mother. Her husband which was a medicine man had a pouch made of leather. It had some kind of powder in it, because he took it from the bag and it looked like dust being spread around. I then awake to a bird pecking at my window. This bird was green and yellow. I didn't know what kind of bird it was so I looked it up in my bird book. It was called a parakeet; they only live in tropical places.

I then walk into the kitchen and start to cook. I then go see if mother is sitting in her rocking chair. She was sitting in her rocking chair and she looked at me and asked if breakfast was ready. That's a good sign when she asks for breakfast in the morning. She also replied I am starving! I replied it is almost done and I fixed all your favorites. I fixed bacon, eggs, potatoes with onions in them gravy and homemade biscuits. I even have raspberry jam and a piece of strawberry pie saved for mom.

I set the table and secretly made a plate for Lone star. I didn't want them to meet him yet, because I didn't know what they would think of him. I then go to the barn and give Lone Star his breakfast. I looked at first after climbing the loft and he was praying. He stopped praying when he heard me and I said here is breakfast. He had a look in his eyes like I was the first white person to care about him.

Lone Star ate real fast like he was really hungry. I then waited for the plate and told him I would be back later. He replied I will wait for you.

I went into the house and called everyone to eat. Joe John and my father ate real fast, because they had to go to town. After Joe John and My father left I cleaned the dishes. Then I go to the barn and talk to Lone Star. We talked about why I moved here from New Jersey. My mother's health was failing her and we had to leave to be in a warmer climate. Lone Star talked to me about great healers in his tribe that could help my mother. He then said he had to go back home.

We go around the barn after climbing out of the loft and glory and behold my little sister Mary sees us. She is always snooping and getting into my things. My mother tells Mary all the time curiosity killed the cat. I guess it is old wives tell to stop snooping so much. Now I wonder what I am going to have to do to get my sister to not tell. I usually have to make a bargain, but when I do she is good at not telling on me.

Lone Star Mounts on his horse and rides away. His horse is white and black. The horse is so pretty with its long hair. I then take my little sister Mary for a walk and a talk. I asked her what it would take for her to keep her mouth shut about Lone Star. She said a bag of gum drops and a Hershey chocolate bar. I replied o.k. I was still little nervous, but that o.k., because I trusted her hundreds of times and she never squealed.

As I cooked diner I pondered on Lone Star and wondered when he would come back. Dad, Joe and John finally come. They are laughing and kidding around, because they have a big job coming up. It will make them a lot of money. It is a big trip moving cattle from Florida to New Jersey. We all ate and went to bed.

I awake to a Parakeet pecking on my window. I guess it is my new alarm clock. I went to the barn and Lone star was there. I asked him to come in and eat breakfast. My dad and brothers left early again.

Lone star comes into the house and he sits at the table, while I cook. My little sister Mary is sitting at the table also. She giggles a lot and makes a statement, he is here again! I replied is it any of your business? Mom is up at this time and tells Mary to eat and mind her own business. Mom is a warm and peaceful person she tells Lone star he is welcomed here any time and he looks at her and smiles.

We finished eating and Lone star mounts on his horse and leaves, but the next day returns. I hear a knock on the door and it was Lone star. I ask him to come in and eat. Joe,

John and Dads eyes looked like they had been frightened by something. They watch Lone star for a while and then lone star finishes eating. He gets up and walks to the door. As we walk outside he asks me if I could meet him at the waterfall a few miles down the road. I replied! Yes I will come and meet you. Then Joe made a smart statement. You're not getting sweet on an Indian is you. I just gave him a dirty look. My dad just looked at me and said I just have to be careful. You really don't know him. I quickly changed the subject. I asked how their trip was.

Mom spoke up and replied he is welcomed in my house anytime. My mother is a very good judge of character. I was done eating and I went outside and saddled up my horse for the trip to the waterfall. It is hot here so I make sure I have plenty to drink. Rhubarb punch is great for your thirst my aunt mama Nicolas use to make it for us in North Carolina all the time. It is great it has pineapple juice along with rhubarb in it. I told mom and everyone goodbye and they told me to be careful. I galloped away and made it pretty quick to the waterfall. When I arrived he was at the very top of the waterfall on top of the cliff. What a pretty picture it was to see his black shining hair in the sun. His dark skin like copper and body built like a warrior. He seen me and dived in to the crystal clear water.

I then dismounted my horse and climbed to the top so I could join him. I took my clothes off except my top and underwear and dived in to. We swam for a long while. We played tag and embraced each other a lot. The roses were so fresh and pretty that the sent was so great for this occasion. We drank rhubarb punch and I think is a little fermented. Then darkness started to come real fast like a storm was brewing. We mounted on the horses, because Lone star said we need shelter fast.

He took us to a cliff in the rocks and we went under the cliff and found shelter. It stormed so bad that the thunder sounded like trumpets and the lighting was like shooting stars. He held me and Lone star took a blanket and wrapped it around me. We decided to stay their all night the storm was so bad we could look down and see the river rise.

The next morning the sun had a rainbow shining from it and the heat was so warm. We said our goodbyes with a hug and a kiss then we went our

Separate way.

I get back home Mom and everyone was so worried, but so relieved I was alright. They couldn't stop telling me they love me. It's something when danger comes to life that is when you're shown the most love. That's why you should never take life for granted. Always tell everyone everyday how much you love them, because life has no promises. After this time I then sat by myself and read my poem.

Life Has No Promises

> One day it's raining and one day it snows. One day it's cloudy and one day the wind blows. Everything is so unpredictable in this world in which we live, but we all know from the day we are born, time is running out. From one day to the next we do not know what the future holds. But for sure who ever is born must one day die. Life is just like the wind. You never know when it is going to blow. Everything has its season - a season to bloom, a season to fall, a season to grow and a season to die. God made everything in rhythm with his nature. That's why life has no promises and we can't predict tomorrow, for we do not know if tomorrow will come.

Days went by and no sign of Lone star and my brothers Joe and John are getting ready with my dad to go and take cattle and sheep to New Jersey. My little sister Mary is going to New Jersey to stay with my sister Karolin. She just had two twin boys and she needs a lot of help. My sister all together has six children. Her husband has a general store and his name is Daniel. Their children are Lynsy, Robbie, Phalesia, Kris, Kurt, and Katie. Their all loved by me, every night I say payers for all my nieces and nephews. So she is going to help with the twins. I helped Mary pack and told her I love her and I gave her a pretty handkerchief. That was given to me years ago from a church Lady sister Lynsy. She is from Jamaica and she works on a big farm for an elderly couple in New Jersey. The Handkerchief always seemed to bring good luck. I told Mary to write me and keep in touch.

My Dad is taking 100 sheep and 200 cattle to New Jersey. I just said good luck and be safe; see you when you get back. Dad just said take care of mom and he picked her up off the ground hugged and kissed her like he was never going to see her again. I then ran into the house and told my sister wait a minute. I went to my chest and found a heart shaped locket that I bought her for Christmas. I was saving it for her. I gave it to her and she cried, because she always wanted one. We said our goodbyes and they left. I waved goodbye and mom like always started to cry.

I bought that locket at the Berlin auction in New Jersey along with a 1740's wedding dress. I swore I would never wear the wedding dress until I find Mr. Wright. It's all lace and comes down in layers like an old fashion dolls dress. That day was sad, but also great, because of the silence Joe and John wasn't fighting and my little sister wasn't around to pick on me all the time. I and mom could finally have quality time with each other. We went for a walk and found an orange tree. Not just an orange tree a honey bell orange tree, my favorite oranges in the whole world. They are as sweet as honey and the juice is thick like honey, but their oranges. I like to make orange marmalade and orange coconut cakes out of them. I also make orange syrup to go on pancakes. Mom helped me pick the oranges and we made orange jelly. I also butchered a hen and mad mom a nice orange baked garnish hen with mashed potatoes and baby carrots.

Mom just loved diner so much that she went outside in the rocking and fell fast asleep. I heard the sounds of nature that night the owls and the frogs and also the wild wolfs howled almost all night long. The stars glittered like diamonds in the sky. Then I asked mom to wake up and she did. She went to bed and fell fast asleep.

The next morning my alarm clock the parakeet woke me up and a knock on the door I heard. I answered the door and he startled me I didn't expect him. It was Lone star, I just kept smiling at him until I seen a man dressed in buffalo skin and a woman dressed in white buck skin. Lone star spoke and said that his father and mother were here to heal my mother. As I asked them to come in with no hesitation I walked into my mother's room as they followed me. My mother looked at us with tears in her eyes like she felt they came to help her. I and Lone star left his mother and father alone with her. Lone Star meditated as I shut my eyes and prayed.

Lone star's parents came out as my mother laid on the bed fast asleep. Lone star's father said let her sleep. He spoke she is being healed. From my mother's facial expression she was very happy and in the spirit world. Tears were in my eyes and I embraced Lone star's mother and said thank you.. I asked if they would stay and eat they replied we must go. Lone star and his parents left and all I could believe is that my mother is well. I sat on the porch for hours. Not even being worried, because I knew God brought my mother's healing to her in a mysterious way. God works in mysterious ways and not our ways as we wish he would. God can use all kinds of instruments for his glory. Who are we I say to myself to show the almighty God how to heal and do things. We are all just sand that goes back to sand in the end. Where it is powerful is that we all have souls and our souls, but not our body's go back to the creator. That is God, because he gave us all a soul.

Later that evening I watched the sunset as it looked red orange and yellow like a fire burning in the sky. I could feel the heat from it all around me. As I heard footsteps I turned and seen my mother walking out the porch door with a smile and a strength of healing on her face. She took a deep breath and looked at the sunset and replied this is a good day for god's grace to be upon me. She said I have my healing and I praise the creator today. I am going to make an orange coconut cake. She looked at me with tears in her eyes and be embraced each other with a strong hug. She replied I claim my healing today.

Mom made an orange coconut cake; I made orange juice and ginseng tea. We sat and talked about old times and laughed. Mom replied laughter is good for your soul and we laughed again. Mom said it is the beginning of healing. Mom stayed up late with me that night. We looked at the stars and we seen a falling star and wished that dad, Joe and john would make it safely back home.

Meanwhile my dad, Joe, John, and Mary made it safe to New Jersey. Mary unpacked and seemed very happy to be with Karolin. They were always pretty close. My dad and brothers sold all the cattle and sheep. They decided to not stay and get on the horses and leave, because dad was always worrying about mom. They made it all the way down to Virginia a place called The Star Dust Saloon. They walk in and theirs dancing and the aroma of good T Bone steak. A big bar and that attracted them, because Joe and john like to drink. Dad he likes a few to, but not around mom. Dad, Joe and John sit down at the bar and order shots of Jack Daniels. They love their Whiskey and which was a nice smooth beer called Samuel Adams. A little old man with guns on his side comes up to dad and asks him to join in a card game. He said ok, because dad is real good at playing cards. Joe and John stays at the bar drinking for a while and then two saloon girls came up to them. One called Dolly which was blonde for Joe and one called Leona a dark haired girl for John. They went off up stairs and rented a room for the night. They call those girls the ladies of the nights.

The next day dad woke up hung over after playing cards most of the night. Joe and John woke up wrapped around their ladies of the night and they got up kissed them told them by and went down stairs. Dad was already there at the table eating his famous ham and eggs. Joe and John ordered steak and eggs and dad asked where they were all night. Joe and John just looked at each other with a smile on their face. They had to of gotten lucky. Dad asked Joe why his hair was all messed up that he looked like he went through a stampede. Joe just looked down and john started laughing and staid yea from the sound of it I think around 3:00 o'clock in the morning he did go through a stampede. Then dad new right away they were with the saloon girls. They all just looked at each other and laughed. They finished eating and mounted on the horses. The girls came out on the balcony outside and waved good bye as they said you all come back here ya'll hear. Dad looked at Joe and John and said I am still wondering where you boys spent the night and laughed. They rode for a while and they mounted off their horses and went down by the water. John picked up Joe and threw him in the water. Joe was mad calling him a Jack Ass in the mud. Then Joe found a frog and slipped it in his saddle bag before they left the water. Dad just said you boys try to get along we only have a little further to go.

Then the frog jumped out of Joe's saddle bag and jumped on the horses head. The horse wouldn't stop bucking up and down it took Joe for a ride he would never forget. It looked like we were at Cow Town in New Jersey at the Rodeo. John deserved it for all the times he picked on

Joe. John called Joe dumb ass and Joe just laughed. John's bottom hurt all the way home.

I awake to foot prints in the house my bird didn't wake me this morning. I was wondering why! I get up Joe, John and dad is home. I hugged them and asked if the ride was rough and me and dad laughed and replied ask john if his ride was rough. He looked real sore and he went and lay down on his stomach on his bed. I just started breakfast and mom walked out of the room with radiance and a glow of beauty on her face. Dad got up and embraced her kissed her and said you look great. Dad new Wright away something was different about her. Dad asked what we were up to and mom changed the subject by, does anyone want a piece of orange coconut cake. Everyone said yes mom and mom cut the cake and served it. Dad started asking questions about what happened when they were gone. I told him Lone star and his mother and father came over and prayed over mom. Mom claims her healing and she has felt good ever since. Tears started flowing down dads face, because he does have faith in God, but also in mom's word.

Then John and Joe start talking about the ride to change the subject. I am sure country boys always show their true feelings in private. I just walked out and started looking for my parakeet. I looked in the barn loft first, because it seems like everything hides there. I thought I seen my bird, but this one was blue. I look on the rafter and found a nest with five baby parakeets in it. They were so small just like a dime chirping so loud. The mother seemed protective, but then my parakeet showed up and landed write on my shoulder. She then backed off a little and sensed I wasn't there to harm them. I told my parakeet I am so happy by petting his feathers. He gave me a kiss on my cheek. Later I brought up a pan of water for them. I didn't see Lone star in fact I didn't see him for a long time. Mom and dad continually talked about going back to New Jersey. I came out and told them I wanted to stay. Joe and John want to go back to New Jersey.

The next morning mom gets up real early, but dad, Joe and John are already gone. They took off to town to buy supplies. I wake up in the morning on my own, because my parakeet is still occupied with his family. I walk into the living room and mom is making three blankets and I asked her who she was making the blankets for? She replied! Ones for Lone star's mother ones for Lone star's father and ones for Lone star. I also have some meats and other supplies for them. I made two orange coconut cakes and wild plum jelly. I told her she was doing too much and she replied! Do what I ask you to do! I said yes mom anything you want me to do I will do. Mom said as soon as I am done find Lone star load up the wagon and take these supplies to his family. I mounted on my horse and went to the falls where we always met. For some reason if we were really desperate to find each other we could.

I arrive at the falls and glory and behold he sits at the top of the falls waiting to jump in until I said, Hey! Lone star you have to come with me. Wright away he came with me after jumping into the water it was a very hot day. I actually would have loved to go swimming, but I always obeyed my mother. We get back to the farm and we go inside. Joe, John, and dad still aren't back yet. Mom said she is finished and she told me what blanket was which. Lone star's mothers blanket was light blue with a white dove. His father's was dark blue with a buffalo and Lone star's was dark blue with stars a moon and a wolf on it. They were so pretty mom did a good job. I could tell Lone star was pleased.

I followed my mother's instructions by loading all the supplies on the wagon. Hooked up my horse and went for the journey to the reservation where he lived. We road for a long time we put Lone star's horse on the back, so he could ride with me on the wagon. We stopped occasionally to water and feed the horses. I knew from how far we have traveled I would have to spend the night.

We finally arrive and I see such beautiful teepees of pretty colors of red, blue, yellow and black. The grass was greener here and it felt so peaceful, like the land was never touched. The river that ran half way around the reservation was crystal clear, just like glass. I thought it just seemed like heaven so pure and uncontaminated. The Indian women were cooking and the Indian men were cutting alligator. We stop the wagon and Lone star goes to his parents. They are pleased that I came to see them.

We start unloading the blankets, along with five chickens, three pigs. The men took the animals probably to butcher them. Lone star's mother took me in the Teepee and I showed her the three blankets. I told her my mother was very pleased that you came and heal her. She was so amazed at the design that my mother made for her. She tried the orange coconut cake and couldn't get enough of it. They cooked alligator and for the first time I tried it. It tastes just like chicken.

They played their drums and Lone star danced for a long time around a great bomb fire. At times the fire looked like it reached the stars. He looks like a great warrior already, but he is still a boy like I am a girl. It takes time to grow up and find your place in life. Night time came to the point where everyone went to sleep and his mother told Lone star to make a bed for me. I felt excepted here like this was my home, but this one Indian girl looked at me as if she was jealous of me. His mother noticed and told me don't worry we asked Lone star to marry her and he won't marry her. This one Indian man that was called a great hunter kept telling hunting stories about how the alligator wouldn't come out of the whole. How his arm was almost bitten off when it came charging at him. How one time he fell in the water off of the canoe to get the alligator and the alligator rolled with him until he cut its throat. I would never want to make him mad he seems like a mean Indian. These Indians were never defeated by American soldiers these Indians that kill big snakes and alligators are the Seminole Indians. Lone star finally makes two places to sleep a bed for me and one for him beside each other.

Meanwhile at home Joe, John and dad get home from town. Mom is peeling potatoes and dad asks what she is doing? He doesn't stop from there, he tells her she needs to rest and stop doing everything. Then he asks where I was? She says she went to drop off some supplies for me. She went to Lone star's family's place and dad replied nothing better not happen to her.

Back at the reservation Lone star and I are looking up at the sky and I told him they look like diamonds and he asked what a diamond was and I said real clear shiny rocks that you can see threw that is worth a lot of money. He said one day I'll take you to my special place that no one knows about .This place has those same rocks. I said o.k. He said, but it is our secret. We then talk about the creator how much beauty he created. Lone star said my eyes are pretty and we fell fast asleep.

I awake to water being thrown in my face. It was that jealous Indian girl. She threw water on Lone star and he became mad and yelled at her. He said leave us alone. She ran away into the woods. After getting up and eating fried bread with my mother's wild plum jelly on it and drinking ginseng tea, we get into the wagon and go back to my house. They all waved good bye and Lone star's mother hugged me and said what will be child will be. We saw eagles flying up above our heads reuniting their love. They fly down to the water attached and just before they come close to the water they let go of each other. It reminds me of how a married couple has an anniversary every year. We seen a fawn, but not the mother and it followed us for a while like it was lost. Then we look behind and see the mother chasing the fawn back to where they hide. Lone star is very smart in a lot of ways.

We get back to the farm and dad was out on the porch. Lone star left without saying hi or by. I guess he doesn't feel like he fits sort of how I feel around that jealous girl. Joe and John were rounding up live stock I guess they will leave soon. Dad asks if I was o.k. I said yes and he smiled and gave me a big hug. I guess dads love for their little girls is sometimes tough love. I go into the kitchen and mom said that their leaving tomorrow morning. I started to cry, because I have always been there for her, my dad and brothers and sisters. Breaking away hurts so badly sometimes, but I am growing up and I need my own life. I go to my room and write this poem.

Departure

Oh how I miss your face being in a unity in which a circle connects the hand shake that sends a message which sends a distance, but a forever bond in our hearts. No matter what distance there is, a forever bond will be. No matter what life brings in our relationship, our strength from God will strengthen us every day. No matter what distance there is between us, in spirit we will always feel unity, because where there is a family circle it never ever dies.

Mom comes in, reads what I wrote and cried. She said I will miss my little girl, because she is my special little girl that God gave me. Dad comes in and says it's raining more in here than outside. It's not like you're never going to see each other again. Night fall came and it was still raining I know in my mind that loneliness will become my best friend. I lie awake for a while and wonder what my life will be like soon. I get up and look in my chest. The wedding dress I bought at nine years old is still waiting for the Wright man in my life. So I write this poem about the wedding dress.

The Wedding Dress

I ponder on this white dress that someday I will wear just for the man that I love. Years of waiting as my heart grows fonder of a man that one day will come for me at last Sunset and moonlit nights looking up at the stars, wondering where he is. I still believe in true love even thou this world seems like there is

> none. No matter what comes I will wait as a princess, lost in a world with no fate hoping and praying for her prince to come. I put on this wedding dress a thousand times a year, practicing a dance that one day I will dance with him. Painted skies of love from my creator above hoping one day that he will bring my prince my way, but as I think, maybe it should be his way. A white horse and a carriage I always dreamed of, but I would settle for just love without a pretty painted picture. As a young girl my hopes and dreams were shattered, but as a wise woman maybe they will finally appear. Hoping and praying to wear my wedding dress soon.

After writing my poem a knock on my window was pretty hard. I go to the window and find my very wet parakeet. The poor little thing, I felt so sorry for him. He is probably wondering why I haven't come to see his family. I took my handkerchief and wrapped him up and put him to bed with me. He stayed with me all night. I'll go see his family tomorrow.

I awake to the sun shining in my face; because I felt

the heat of the sun I opened my eyes. My parakeet Sony sits on my shoulder and I go to the barn to see his family. I climb up in the barn loft and I see the sun shining threw and five green and blue parakeets flying all around. I was so surprised. I opened up the barn window and the mother took them threw it to teach them to fly. I and my parakeet watched and then he took off with them. I watched and then I went to the house, because mom, dad, Joe and john are leaving me today.

I started to help mom pack, while mom cooked bacon and eggs with gravy and biscuits. We all sat down for the last time to eat and they had already loaded up the wagons. We were all very quiet; I guess that means we will miss each other. We were all done and mom gathered a few more things and they all went to the porch. I started to cry and mom started to cry and we hugged goodbye. I said I would write and they helped mom on the wagon. My dad hugged me with tears in his eyes and said be careful. My brothers hugged me and didn't show tears, but later by themselves cowboys sometimes break down and cry. I said a prayer and asked God to watch over everyone as they were leaving. They said they will send telegrams every few weeks' western union.

They left me fifty cattle, fifty sheep; five horses, ten pigs and I still have my bane roosters and hens. They multiply real quickly! I was all alone except for Lone star, but I never knew when he would come around to see me. I was in hopes that I would meet the true love of my life one day. I kept my self busy by collecting eggs and making my jelly and jams. I would sale them at the general store in town. I made orange and strawberry syrup for the diner in town. I sold cattle and my prize roosters and hens. I did good for myself as far as making money.

Today while sitting on the porch I heard a horse, it was Lone star. He said that he had to come and tell me of a dream he had. He said beware of a man in black that he can't be trusted. He seemed very concerned about me. I made us diner and after we went on the porch and heard the coyotes howling. It was a full moon and it was so pretty with the stars shining at night. He spent the night in my mother's bed. When I awakened to the sun in my eyes, I went to my mother's room where Lone star slept and he was gone. There was an eagle feather on my mother's pillow. I took it in my hands and it felt like a lucky charm or a four leaf clover.

Loneliness is my friend just like I said it would be. Lone star has a responsibility to his mother and father.

That night there was a knock on my door and hoping to

see Lone star it wasn't. I opened the door and a man in black almost passing out said he has been shot. A loving person and trusting I let him come in. I boiled water and took a bottle of rubbing alcohol to kill the germs. I took a sharp knife and took out the bullet. I then sewed the wound up and gave him some of my homemade brandy that I made years ago in New Jersey. I also have huckleberry brandy and blue berry brandy. He really liked the brandy and then he fell fast asleep.

The next morning he woke up and I fixed him some Campbell's chicken noodle soup out of a can called Campbell. They say it is the best canned soup around. After a few days he was gone after I went into town for supplies. In my mind I kept remembering what Lone star told me about the man in black. Sometimes feelings get in the way of your vision when you're young. I never even asked the guys name. After I got back from town he was still gone and I went in the house to put supplies away and then I hear a knock on the door. He said my name is Charles Lang and I hated to meet you the way we met. Could I come in and talk. I said yes!

He came in and I gave him a cup of coffee and orange coconut cake. He also started sweeping the floor and helping me with my chores. Then he asked if he could take me to the beach. I said sure and he already had a picnic basket in the wagon waiting for us. He was so sure of his self I thought. We made it to the beach and I was hungry. We put the blanket down and he started opening the basket and getting out the plates. It seemed like he thought of everything from fried chicken to mashed potatoes to corn on the cob and biscuits. I thought to myself and I didn't even have to cook.

After we ate we made a big sand castle and went swimming. I found three lobster three dozen clams and three dozen of oysters. We put them on the wagon in a tub with water and we made our way back home before dark. We cooked all of the seafood and melted sweet butter for their taste. It was so great that night to have fresh seafood. They say the way to a women and man's heart is threw their stomach. He opened up a bottle of red wine we drank and danced to the sounds of the owls and the howling of the coyotes.

He left that night and didn't come back for a few days later. When he did come back he was at the door with a dozen of red roses. He asked if he could come in and I agreed that he could come in and have coffee. I asked him to stay for diner and he did. I made Italian hoagies just like mom use to. He asked what it was, because he never had one. I cut all the vegetables fresh from the garden. The meat was stored in my ice box and it was fresh. He started to eat it and he just loved it so much he asked for another one. Then he said he needed to go home and go to bed. He picked me up off of the floor kissed me and gave me a big hug then told me he would see me tomorrow. Then I was alone again to the sounds of my roosters crowing hens cackling and cows mooing. Then I sat on the porch in the rocking chair and went fast to sleep. I then dream of a man in black with a gun and it was pointed to me. I also dream of a wagon and a baby falling out of it. I couldn't tell if she was dead or alive. I awake from my dream with Sony my bird on my head. It was night time so I went inside and fell to sleep. I couldn't sleep to good and I tossed and turned all night.

I awake to the sun shining in my face now I know why they call this place the sun shine state. Someone is at the door and I open it. It was Charles Lang he picks me up kisses me and carries me and then makes his way to the bedroom then puts me on the bed. He starts to make love to me and I just couldn't resist the passion he had for me. It's something when you're young and you get caught up in life's passions, fears of being alone and a small letter word that is very dangerous called love. Then with a surprise he asked to move in. I was unsure in my mind, but I decided to say yes!

Everything seems like its working out o.k. but I can see there is just something about him that doesn't meet my eye. Three months later a knock on the door and Charles answers it. He opens the door and Lone star is standing there. Charles says some Indian is at the door and I walked to the door and said this is Lone star all Lone star did was look at me and say beware of the man in black and walked away with disappointment. I then felt so alone and hurt that I lost my very best friend in the whole world.

That's a crazy Indian Charles said! I said he is my friend and don't you ever say that to him ever again. That was the first time he ever seen me mad, because I slammed the door and he knew to leave me alone. A month later my friend didn't come and I knew something was wrong after I started throwing up. I had to of conceived in my bedroom experience. I thought to myself I am not married and mom and dad is going to disown me. God I pray you forgive me for my passions and being in this human form. I just have to make my wrong write that is what the Bible says if you commit a sin ask forgiveness and make it right and God will forgive you.

Charles came to me and said he had to leave, because his

mother was sick. I didn't believe him when he told me that. He left and he said he would be back in a few days and he didn't come back at all. It was three months passed and he still wasn't back. Loneliness is my friend, but I also have a permanent friend that's coming soon. I had a dream that I had a son and I called him Charles Joseph. Lone star must have watched from a distance, because my chores of feeding the animals were always done for me when I would get up in the morning. Finally Lone star couldn't resist and he came up to the porch. He knew right away I was pregnant.

Meanwhile Charles Lang was doing time in jail for theft down in West Palm Beach Florida. They have him breaking rocks on a chain gang. He had stolen ten horses and almost killed a guy when he tried to take his pocket watch. They said the guy just wouldn't let go of his pocket watch. Come to find out he stole that guys pocket watch years ago and the guy noticed it and he wanted it back.

Lone star and I talked and I cried and said I was so sorry that I didn't listen to him. Lone star just said friends stay closer than brothers and sisters after months of Lone star staying with me in my mother's room and helping me. All of a sudden the pains start to come. Lone star picked me up and put me to bed. He traveled as fast as he could to the reservation, but after Lone star found out I was pregnant he told his mother. So all this time his mother was on alert to come, so a fourth of the way to the reservation his mother was almost to the house. Lone star and his mother met a little ways down the trail. Indians know things that other nationalities don't know, because of the spirit world. Lone star and his mother came back just in time to deliver my son. Lone star held my hand all the way. I delivered in seven and a half hours. He was six pounds two ounces and nineteen and a half inches long.

Lone star stayed with me for eight months he fathered Charles Joseph J.R Lang. Charles didn't know his real father until one day. Out of the blue a knock on the door I opened it and it was Charles Lang. I let Charles Lang back in my life for a second chance, but I hope I don't live to regret this.

Lone star stepped aside and went back to the reservation, disappointed again. I often wondered why I and lone star was never more than friends, but the chemistry was there. Charles Lang helped on the farm and often went into town and came back with a lot of money. I finally asked where the money came from, but he said just some odd jobs. He seemed like a good father to Charles J.R, but Charles always asked for Lone Star. Charles J.R always seemed very lonely at times, so I gave in and nine months later I gave birth to a six pond two once baby girl. I named her TaLaceya Ann.

Charles Lang S.R wanted to marry me, but I refused to marry him. It made him angry and he started walking to the barn. He stayed in the barn all night. So when morning came he sat down and ate breakfast. Nothing else was said about marriage. It was about three weeks after Tabethas birth and I decide to take us all into town. We went in the wagon with my horse attached. On the way we saw an alligator along the side of the road. Charles J.R asked what it was. Charles S.R replied, an alligator son! The first time I ever heard him call Charles J.R son. I smiled thinking that he was making some kind of effort to be a father. We finally arrive into town. I ask Charles S.R to stay on the wagon and watch TaLaceya until I go into the general store with Charles J.R. He said that he would, but then when I went into the store me and Charles was counting out some candy that he wanted I looked out the window and seen a man on a horse riding crazy threw town. All of a sudden my horse gets spooked and takes off a little. TaLaceya is thrown from the wagon to the ground and I run out to get her. I pick her up and she's not breathing and the Doctor comes out and helps me perform C.P.R. Doctor Jacobson looked at me and said I feel a heartbeat and all of a sudden she lets out a cry. I look and see through the window Charles Lang S.R drinking and playing cards I was so out raged I just Got in the wagon after the Doctor told me to take her home and keep her awake that she might have a concussion. She is so small that she might develop neurological damage, because of the trauma to the brain. One of the men came out of the bar and said the man on the horse was a drunk that lost in a card game with Charles Lang S.R years ago. I just got in the wagon as fast as I could and left to go home.

I get home and do everything the doctor told me to do. It was hard staying up all night and Charles S.R must have found out what had happened, because he didn't come home. Nightfall came and Charles J.R asked if his sister was o.k.? I said I hope so son just pray for your sister. I took him to the bedroom said a prayer of hope for God to make his sister o.k. and kissed him, I then put him to bed. I stayed up all night and when the sun came up there was a knock on the door. It was Doctor Jacobson and I embraced him. I said I kept her up all night and gave her Tylenol for children. He said you're a good mother Lacey and I admire you for your courage, but I read up last night on trauma and your daughter by checking her over has three bruises to her brain and a bruise on her spine. She might develop cerebral palsy, but time will tell. She might seem sluggish at times, but if she doesn't walk by the time she's 18 months she will have cerebral palsy. She will have problems walking, talking and her motor skills will be off set. I broke down and I cried out and said God why! My daughter Lord why! My daughter Doctor Jacobson said you have to be strong for TaLaceya. He then hugged me and said if you need anything contact me. From time to time I will come and check on you and your children. I knelt down and prayed this prayer.

A Prayer for a Desperate Mother

> Dear Lord I pray that you will help me through this assignment, for I will never blame anything in this life that seems like a tragedy or a misfortune on you. I know this is a faith builder with a blessing in the end, but please help me through this pain. Guide me in a way to carry her over this great mountain and in the end bring healing to her life. Lord you said you would never leave or forsake me. I know I am never alone.

I sit and cry, but then feel great warmth around me, like a blanket that is soft like wool. I then know that God is with me. I remember this warmth when I was in a bath tub at four years old rinsing my head with a glass. Skeet was in the bath tub with me. I drop the glass and push away from the glass, but I fell back on the glass and cut my back. I told my sister I was going to heaven and she screamed, because of all the blood. My mother heard the screams and it scared her and she ran as fast as she could. She came and took me out of the tub and told me to hold on. She cried out to God and I felt a wool blanket cover me. I woke up in Dr. Shepherd's office; he said you're lucky to be alive! You almost bleed to death, but God must be with you. He just smiled with that great heavenly smile and told my mom to keep me on my stomach and keep me warm.

I know this is going to be tough, but I know God is with me. I fix a cup of coffee and I hear a knock on the door it was Lone star. It's something how Lone star knows when something is wrong with me and the children. He is the greatest friend I have ever known. I ask him in and he gives me a great hug and me I just cry, because I have never had such a faithful friend. Charles runs straight for him and he picks him up like always and rubs his head. I didn't know when Charles Lang S.R would show up, but Lone star seemed unworried. Why should he be Lone star is a young warrior always ready for battle, but very humble he never causes trouble for me.

My family still doesn't know about the children I know they will feel ashamed of me, because I am not married. So I will send the information to my sister Skeet, she will tell them in a way I hope won't hurt them and I won't be disowned. I know I should give my parents more credit, but it is the 1800s. Some religions kill women for adultery. So I ask Lone star to watch the children while I go to town and send a telegram western union to my sister Skeet. It reads Dear Skeet your little has had a son two years ago and recently had a daughter which was in a very bad accident. I also am not married and the man Charles Lang S.R left and I heard that he goes to jail a lot. I can't see why I was taken in by that bad man, but I was and I am sorry. Please tell mom and dad my story in a way they won't disown me. I love you and hope you will write me and keep in touch. My little girl might develop cerebral Palsy sincerely your little sister Eliza Lacey.

As I walk out of the Western Union to get on my horse a man ran up to me from the saloon. He said Last night in Virginia City Charles Lang was shot and drug threw the town by a wagon train. He gave me the News paper and told me he was sorry. It seemed like everyone knew I was with him. My reputation was just ruined. I was sorry inside, but then again relieved that he was out of my life for good. He was a coward and I knew it from the beginning, but was in denial. I took off on my horse so fast and so free it seemed like I was running a race for my life or my salvation. In my mind I am a single mother, but God said he fathers the fatherless. In my mind on the back road where I traveled a lot where there was nothing, but beauty I prayed dear God help me, but most of all save my soul and keep me and the children safe.

I arrived back at the farm and Charles J.R came running to me. He knew something was wrong, but I couldn't tell him. I went in and started cooking and cleaning the house to try to leave things in the past.. Night fall came and I sat out on the porch listening to the sounds of the night. Sometimes the sounds of night soothe my soul along with looking at the stars at night.

I then go in to my room and fall fast asleep. Lone Star is already asleep from taking care of the children all day while I went into town. The next morning I get up and start cooking breakfast, but first I check on TaLaceya and Charles they are still asleep. I fix breakfast, I leave it on the stove for them and I drink a cup of coffee on the porch. Lone star is already up feeding the animals. My pet parakeet is flying with his family today. I look up in the sky and see them.

I then see a horse and a man riding toward the house with a news paper in his hand. He said excuse me Lacey, I heard of your tragedy and feel that you should read this paper and then he didn't say a word and left just as fast as he came in. Lone star watched from a distance and wondered what went wrong. I read the paper about a man called Charles Lang shot by Billy the kid and another known gun slinger with no name. They then after shooting him drug him in the streets of Virginia City. At that moment I felt so alone, but relieved that I don't have a dishonest man in my life no more. I will go on threw life baring the reproach of an unwed mother. Days went by and Lone star new that trouble had come, but still he was a loyal friend to me. He helped TaLaceya by putting little sand bags on her legs and balancing her while she walked. He put her on the horse that he had for her. The offspring of our horses breaded and made a beautiful spotted black and white stallion. He is so gentle and so pretty.

Time goes on and my children see Lone star as a father figure until one day his parents come to see him. I go in the house and then Lone star came in and hugged me goodbye. I watch him and his family leave, but I knew that he had to eventually go back and marry someone from his own tribe. It broke my heart, but I was happy for him, because he helped me and my children. Charles is five and TaLaceya three she can't walk completely straight, but better than being paralyzed. I keep working with her like Lone star did. Charles helps her all the time by walking her with her hand. He is such a good son and faithful son.

I then go into town to get my mail and a man from Western Union came out and told me there is a message for me. The message was from Skeet. Dear Lacey you have to come to Wisconsin, because there is a man called Adam Wenk that owns Strawberry Farms winery. He isn't married and is looking for a wife. I have done his hair at the Barber shop for two years. He is a good man and he has never been married. I then get my mail, buy some food from the General store and make my way back home.

All the way home I kept thinking of the two men that came to me with newspapers about Charles Lang S.R. I guess sometimes it is very hard to let go. I thought about my sister and decided it would be best for me to leave. I prayed all the way home asking God to help me on my trip to Wisconsin. I hear it is very cold their and it snows all of the time.

I arrive home and the children are fine and Charles is

outside picking up oranges while TaLaceya is trying to peal one. That is a good sign at least she knows something is inside to eat. I go in and try to figure out how to coordinate my journey to Wisconsin. I start writing things down and while writing I have decided to sale all live stock and chickens except two hens and a rooster. I should have at least $5,000 dollars to help me get started in Wisconsin. I'll also take Charles horse, mine and TaLaceyas. I decided to leave the birds behind because they need warm weather. I hope Lone star comes and says goodbye.

The doctor came the next morning to see me and we talked about TaLaceya. I told him we were leaving and going to Wisconsin. He said fine, but keeps in touch with me, because with the new medicine and operations coming out it could help TaLaceya. He hugged me and kissed me on the cheek. I then ask him to pin up flyers at the store to sale my animals. Doctor Jacobson said anything for you Lacey. Some people call me Lacey for short. I hope people can come soon to buy. I just need a new change in my life. I miss Lone Star, but I know he has obligations to his tribe. I will miss my great friend, but I am sure in my life time I will see him again.

I waited and had a very rich man show up and buy everything that was for sale. I thanked him for everything.

Now I had enough money to go with. I kept two hens and a rooster of my Bane's, because they multiply fast. I kept two cows and two pigs and three horses, so I can at least keep a farm to make money. I start to pack and tell the children were leaving tomorrow morning for Wisconsin. They are excited, but asked if Lone Star was coming. I said no! He is staying with his tribe, so pack up all the things that are special to you. What a mistake that becomes in our life a little too late.

As dawn fell and as fast as it did it seemed like morning came. The sun shining and birds singing like the heart of nature was bursting into a new beginning. I cooked, fed the children, packed the wagons and left. It was tuff, because I didn't know what was really up ahead. I just decided that I had a vision of a future and I was going to get there.

The first day was rough and Charles kept hiding something. At night I could of sworn I heard birds in my wagon. TaLaceya slept the whole day, because the heat was so unbearable. We found a pond and camped out, but first went swimming. We had fun me and Charles, but TaLaceya stayed close to the beach. Change doesn't seem to bother Charles, but TaLaceya seems a little worried. I wish every day I had a father for them. I know God fathers the fatherless and he will father mine if it has to be that way.

We all ate and we fell asleep. I then heard a sound after a few hours. It was pretty loud so I went for my gun. I didn't wake the children. I went around the back of the wagon and seen a raccoon fighting with another raccoon over my frying pan. They didn't run and they made a friendly sound, so I know what that meant. They had to be the ones that use to get in my pies and cakes when I cooled them on the window seal.

I just left them and looked in the wagon at TaLaceya and couldn't deny that precious little girl her two raccoons. I then feel something on my head and it was my parakeet and under the covers his wife and offspring. Charles has done this one I just hope nothing else appears. I won't scold them Ill just play around and kid with them until they feel guilty enough to tell me. Then I just laugh a little to myself, because I use to do the same thing as a child. I go back to sleep, but first say a prayer. Lord helps me through this journey and protects us.

The second day was nice and the children were up before me, so something is going on. Charles packed up all the stuff and all I had to do was put some cold water on my face and go. He is the man in my life now. Charles always tries to take care of me and TaLaceya. Our life is very different now that we don't have Lone Star. We are watching the eagles teach their young to fly as we travel. I try not to stop too much, because we really have to get there. Night falls again and we make camp by a nice river where the children can take a bath.

Did you ever hear the sound of the coyotes as night fell? They sound so scary, but yet so free and beautiful. Where would the sound of nature be without this in the wilderness? Don't forget the sound of the owls at night and their flashing eyes. I love the sight and sounds of nature, because it keeps night life alive and unique with the stars and the full moon shining down.

Its night time and I made trout for diner. We are nearing Wisconsin, because the temperature is dropping rapidly. Two more nights and we will be in Rhinelander Wisconsin. Today we are in Illinois and there is a lot of rain. If it keeps up I will have to stop and get into the wagon. I can't hardly see threw the water and it scares me, because of the wholes. I don't want to break a wheel or get stuck. I don't have any help, but I do have strong horses. Finally the rain stops God must have heard me. I start looking into the distance and Gods promise which is the rainbow comes out to say hello. I keep going until nightfall and I just park on the side of the road and we all after eating Jerky and canned peaches go fast asleep. I think the children are wondering when we are going to get there.

The next morning my hens had laid six eggs so I made some cheese omelets for us all. We ate and went on our way real quick, because one more night and we will be at my sisters. We traveled all day and then hit the border of Wisconsin the cheese state. The first thing we seen was a bear and the second was about a hundred herds of deer. I then finally knew we were almost in Rhinelander. I put sweaters on the children, because it was about 60 degrees and that is cold for us. As we traveled the temperature dropped even more and it seemed like winter even thou it was just September. I found a place to camp for the night. It was by the lake of the Torches they call it. Then I saw a sign that said Pottawatomie Indian land. The water was crystal clear, but I wondered if these Indians were friendly. I start to hear the sound of the drums and a lot of loud sounds. I then knew I was near their homes and they were having Pow wow. I hope they don't mind me being here. I didn't light a fire I bundled the children up and we ate Jerky, canned fruits and vegetables then we went to sleep.

The next morning I didn't cook I gave the children cookies and some milk and went straight to Kim's. We made it in three hours. I went through the town of Rhinelander like she said and went down a long dirt road. Her house is six bed rooms and she has a big barn. I show up and she's not their there's a note on the door go in and make yourself at home. I fixed diner and unloaded all my stuff and then put the children to bed. I then waited on her porch for her to come home.

With a trail of dust as she always shows up in a blaze of glory, it is my sister Skeet with two guns on her side and the most beautiful black stallion you ever want to see. Her hair cut short and sassy as she always is. She is always the center of attraction and that's fine, because I love her very much. As we hug and cry as always and she checks the children sleeping in their rooms she says she is proud that they are here. She said I can't wait until you meet this man I have done his hair for two years named Adam. He is very handsome and unique, but has lived with his parents all of his life. We had a hot cup of tea and went to bed. The next day I woke up early and cleaned the house. I cooked ham, eggs and put on a pot of coffee. Skeet just grabbed some biscuits, a piece of ham, jumped on her horse and road to her shop.

Little did I know she was working things out to get Adam to her shop, so I could meet him? Well I leave the children sleeping for a while, because their exhausted from the trip. I go exploring and I take plenty of jars with me to pick black berries, blue berries and everything I can find, because the season is almost over. I find a fence and see loads of raspberries, blackberries, blueberries and strawberries. I see a no trespassing sign and I ignore it. I slip over the fence and start picking. I have all the berries I want and I turn around to get back over the fence and a man calls out from the road and said you could at least ask me to pick my berries. I said well I always felt the land was free. Now I am looking at him face to face, but I am still on the fence trying to get unattached, because my dress was caught on a nail. He then said do you need help? Stupid me, said no.! I said I will make you a strawberry pie if you want. He said no harm done just ask next time. While he left and I am still stuck on the fence I lose my balance and fall off the fence. Some of my berries were a little smashed, but most of them were fine, because as I picked I was climbing over the fence and putting them in my saddle bag.

I took off and went Wright home. The children woke up and I fed them. Skeet has a lake so I took the children swimming, but it was freezing cold. She spoke about another lake that the locals all go to called Buck Lake. Maybe we will go sometime and have a picnic. Settling in and trying to fit in is the hardest part. I Hope I never see that guy that caught me picking his berries on his property. I am sort of embarrassed about that, because I didn't know what to say. As I am sitting on the porch my sister said tomorrow I want you at my shop at around 12:00 noon. I want to fix your hair and do your nails. I want you to wear a pretty dress to come and get your hair done. I was sort of suspicious, but I trust my sister's judgment. As I sat on the porch with a cup of hot tea, because I feel the cold hear is sort of different then what I have been use to. Thinking about Lone Star my great friend I saw the Indians in the distance as I left Florida. I didn't wave, but they watched me as I crossed the line and Lone Star was there with his new wife with a child in her. His family seemed relieved, because they marry within their tribe. To keep a strong blood line they must all have an arranged marriage. Even if true love is not found they are to obey their elders. I know I shall always be the one in his heart even thou she is with him every night.

I finally get tired; go to bed and dream of a prince that takes me to a beautiful palace. This man has eyes like the sky on a beautiful sunny day. I then hear my parakeet at the window and I let him in. My little faithful friend that always keeps me company when there is no one else. Today is the day I must go into town and get my hair and nails done. I get up fix breakfast and feed the animals. I then take the children put them in the room with toys and the German shepherd called Bernard and then take off to town. Skeet says if you leave the dog with the children he will kill anything that comes around. I take off on my horse into town hoping to get there on time.

I finally arrive in town; I get off my horse tie her up and walk in Skeet shop. I see a back of a man's head and what beautiful hair he has. Skeet looks up and spins him around toward me and say's Adam I want you to meet my little sister Lacey. Both of his eyes and mine was as big as silver dollars. It was him the guy that yelled at me about the berries. He just looked and replied nice to meet you little lady. Skeet just laughed and I didn't think anything was funny. Then I finally livened up after I looked deep into his eyes, I was startled in a way. His eyes looked just like those snow white doves in New Jersey; I use to see as a child. They were so blue just as blue as the Gulf of Mexico. The water on the Gulf of Mexico is real blue. He asked me if I wanted to have a cup of coffee at the café. I was going to play hard to get. I had enough bad luck with men Good looks and a clean cut can cause a lot of trouble. I replied! I came to get my hair and nails done, I don't have time. His face turned as red as the beets I use to pick in the Garden, in New Jersey. Skeet smiled she knew right away with that sneaky grin on her face, what I was intending to do. So he was done and he left the shop. I finish at the shop and make my way back home. I then find the children and Bernard taking a nap on the floor with blankets. I then heat up leftovers and sit on the porch until they wake up. It's so funny, because Bernard never opens his eyes or barks when I come home. He must have a great six cents, very aware of everything around him.

I am out on the porch just listening to the sounds of nature, as night falls. I am all alone on the porch and I feel like it's a little spooky here in these back woods. The stars are so bright, the moon is so full, and I hear a sound of a coyote. I often wondered about the sound of a coyote, because why would they cry out like the call of the wild. An Indian told me they cry out for their mate. It must be some wild affair that we may not ever understand. Well I hear horse hoofs and their coming pretty quick and loud, so it must be my sister Skeet. Yes! Skeet comes in and says she is so proud of me. She hugged me and said she was tired and she went fast to sleep. I am the only one up so; I put the food away and went to bed myself.

I stayed awake in bed looking at the moon and the stars looking at the big and little dippers thinking of Mr. Adam

Wenk and his beautiful eyes. They were like diamonds, but I still had a guard up thinking I won't pursue him unless he pursues me. I don't want to make another mistake, because I am already a single mother in my twenty's. In the 1800 that is bad news for a woman. The looks you sometimes get when you're out in town. I hold my head high and if the good Lord didn't want me to have my children he wouldn't of given them to me. God says children are gifts and they should be loved. Those words are good enough for me! I fell fast asleep looking at a twinkling star. I dreamed of a vineyard of grapes and roses. I dreamed that Adam Wenk invited me to see his home and life as he has it all set up. Everything in my dream was perfect, because everything had its place to be in. As I love perfection, I also feel imperfection is made to be improved. I awake to a knock on the door and it is about 10:00 o'clock and everyone including my sister Skeet is still asleep. That's not like me to sleep that long I am always up when my Bane rooster crows.

I go to the door and glory and behold who is standing at the door, Adam Wenk his self with those blue eyes asking me if I want to go out and see the country side. I am standing in my night cloths and I don't know what to say, but I responded and said o.k. I will go with you just give me a few minutes and will get ready. He waited and I got dressed in my Levis and a flannel, because it gets sort of nippy after 3:00. I yelled at Skeet watch the children and feed the animals, because I am gone for the day. I saved a nice bottle of Strawberry wine called Strawberry's farm and took it with us. I jumped in the wagon with his help and off we go. He takes me to Lake Superior up near the Canadian border and the beauty was breath taking. I then stuck the Strawberry Farm wine in Lake Superior and waited ten minutes and it was ice cold. He had wine glasses and we had a nice cold drink of wine. I was thirsty, so I drank pretty quick and started talking a lot like us women do on alcohol it sort of makes us have a lose tongue. He helps me off the wagon and puts a blanket down on these beautiful daisies. He then starts talking about his life in Wisconsin. How it was hard living with his parents all these years and never getting married, but he felt obligated to them. They took in two twins from his mother's sister that couldn't take care of them. He felt he had to help raise them, because his parents were getting older. I really felt sorry for him in a great way. He seemed like a good man, but desperate to have a good wife and he told me my children were a plus, because he never wanted his own offspring.

We had a good day and he brought a great basket of

food. It had fried chicken from the Kernels a little restaurant there with chicken and dumplings with biscuits and mashed potatoes. We had raspberry pie for desert and he brought his own bottle of imported wine called pinot gringo. Then night fall came and we made it home at 12:00 midnight. He helped me off the wagon and he kissed me on the cheek. I then walked away after saying thank you for a great day! I went and checked all the rooms and everyone was sleeping. I crawled under my covers after making it to my room. I thought about my great day and then went to sleep, because I was so tired.

Dreams of a wedding and wearing my white lace dress came to my mind carriage and a black stallion pulling me to my destination where I would marry my great prince. I came to a church where roses seemed to be part of my soul for the sent was a fragrance from heaven. It seemed so innocent that the tears began to flow from my face. My daughter TaLaceya and my son Charles was Wright there in the carriage with me. Then a peck from Sony on my face, it awakened me. I hear a knock on the door, for the first time in years, I had over slept.

I put my house coat on and ran to the door and it was Adam Wenk with a dozen of red roses. I accepted them and thanked him. I didn't want to be so quick at inviting him in, but I did anyway.

We had a cup of coffee and I put the roses in a vase my mother had given me that was passed on from her mother called painted glass. It was blue, red and scarlet with a little bit of yellow in it. Adam really thought it matched the occasion. I wondered what the roses were for, but I never asked. He just kept looking at me and finally asked me to come to his house and meet his mother and father. He also had a little surprise for me. I asked what the surprise was and he said it wouldn't be a surprise if I told you. He said I'll go and I'll be back at about five o'clock and I agreed.

Everyone in the house was still sleeping and I picked out my red dress and black shoes to wear for him tonight. I then put on my Levis, boots and sat out on the porch with another cup of coffee. Everyone can have Kellogg's corn flakes with strawberries in it. Kellogg's is a new brand out fortified in vitamins. I just have to milk the cow. Kim has a good cow! She puts out a gallon and half of milk a day. Skeet calls her Sassy, because sometimes she shakes her right back leg and jumps a little when you bother her too much. I try never to go in back of her, because if that cow ever kicks her she could really hurt you.

I go and milk her real quick and I look back, because I felt someone standing in back of me. It was Charles, so I acted like I didn't see him. I squeezed the tit and squirted him with milk then he took off running and I ran after him. He runs pretty fast, but the little guy got a glass of cold water and dumped it right on my head. I tried to get him and he ran back to the barn and hid in the loft. I go in the loft and what a sight to see a pretty colorful web made of wool. I told Charles to come down, because I didn't know if it was a poison spider or what. He finally came out of hiding and we went to the kitchen and poured him a bowl of Kellogg's. TaLaceya gets up and crawls to the table. I put her in the highchair and she starts to eat. It seems like the cold climate is giving her a better appetite. I then pour myself a bowl of Kellogg's and eat with them. I love my little family even thou I wish I had a father for my children. I look at them and start to pray for our food they then fold their hands and bow their head. We don't have much, but I always taught them to pray over their food and to pray every night and thank God for everything you do have.

I told them I have a date to meet Adam's family tonight at five o'clock. They seemed happy and Charles said can we come? I replied not this time Bernard will keep you company. My sister's faithful wolf she found him as a puppy. Skeet said he perfects the farm and everyone in the house. It was something he took a liking to Lacey, so I knew he was a good man. It starts to get later and I get dressed and ready for Adam to come. He shows up and comes in the house to say hello to the children. He picks TaLaceya up and cuddles her. She loved that very much! He then puts out his hand to Charles and Charles smacked his hand. I guess it is telling each other they accept each other. We then get ready and go for a long ride. I saw such beautiful roses and grape vineyards. Come to find out he owns Strawberry farm wines. We first go to the barn and he gave me a glass of strawberry wine. I said this is strawberry and he replied the same strawberries you picked off my land. I laughed and he said I'd better give you a glass before we meet my mother. I wondered what that meant, he just said don't take everything she says to heart. It sort of puzzled me in a way walking up to the, but I give everyone a chance to care for me the way I want to be cared for.

We get to the house and his father comes out first a very tall man and heavy set. He says hello and I could tell he took a liking to me Wright away. He shook my hand and he said you must be Lacey, I replied yes! What a pleasure to see his mother in the kitchen baking an apple pie. She just looked and said you must be Lacey and I replied, yes! I could tell that she liked what she saw, but then the questions were asked about my life. I went around telling her about the children, so I just said I moved here from Florida and they said are you going to be able to adjust to the cold. I said

I could adjust to anything if I have something to stay for. Adam looked at me and I looked at him and then he said lets go it's getting late and we said goodbye it was nice meeting you. They said hope to see you again and I replied of course.

On the ride home I hardly said anything, because I know wants I mention my children, it will be over. They seem like they want their own grandchildren, like blood is thicker than water. I know Adam accepts them he said next time bring the children and don't feel that they won't be excepted as long as I accept them that's all that matters. We finally get home and he kissed me goodnight and left. I walk in the house and find the prettiest sight. The children had fallen asleep on the floor with their heads on Bernard with the fireplace going and them all covered up and sound to sleep. I let them sleep and I went to bed wondering if I was accepted. I often thought of Lone star and his family and not being accepting as far as a wife, but a great friend. Now I am in a different place and have to find acceptance again. I won't have my children hurt for no one. I will take it alone if I have too. I fell asleep and feel great warmth that everything was going to be alright. I say my prayer and God comforts me as I cry myself to sleep.

Insecurity sits in, but hopefully things will work out. I just want a good home for my children. I don't want to parish in this world emotionally with them not having a father. I go to sleep and wake up to a knock on the door. It was Adam and he wanted to talk to me. He wants me to bring the children to see his mom and dad. He had told them about the children. They seemed surprised, he replied, but excepting. First he brought me out side and asked to marry me. He had the biggest star diamond I had ever seen. I accepted Wright away. I said I sure will marry you! We told the children and they smiled, but I could tell that Charles seemed uneasy about it. A mother picks up on those emotions that are hidden in their children. It's a gift us woman have that men don't have as strong sometimes. It is a maternal thing that goes on all the days of our lives. So we all get dressed and I fixed quick egg, cheese and ham biscuits. We get in his black carriage and were off to his parent's house.

On the trip their talks to the children and tells them the names of the animals along the way. I love the eagle that flew over us all the way to his parents, it actually freed me of the in securities I have regarding his parents. We arrive at his parents and they come out of the house with a girl introduced as patsy and another girl with long brown hair called Christina. I liked her best out of all, because at least shell gives you a chance. The other seemed nice, but not willing to give a chance. I met the twins Joe and Josie, Joe is the boy and Josie is the girl. They seemed o.k. except the girl Josie was off Standish. We all sat down for lunch and Adam announced us getting married. Everybody seemed very quiet, but we will all get through it. I want to make it work regardless of all the evil that happened in my life. They all at one time said when is the date? We didn't decide, but Adam said wants to get married January 9, 1860. I agreed and Christina wants to make the flowers out of silk. I was so pleased and then Mrs. Mel ba wants to make the food. They said we can get married at the Baptist church.

I was so happy and felt excepted for the first time. We went home and we told Skeet, and for the first time in her life she felt happiness for me. I am on top of the universe. I start planning to wear my dress and make them part of the wedding. Finally the day has come to walk down that and I show up at the church on time in a white couch. The children ride with me to the church Charles with a worried look and TaLaceya just looking off in the distance. We arrive and we finally are getting ourselves out of the carriage and I meet Adam's sister's husbands for the first time. Tony and Mark were their names. They were very well mannered and very well liked.

I get into the church and everyone was their all my family and all his. The music starts and I look into Adam's eyes and greatness of love I seen for the first time in my life. My father on one side and my son on the other they walk me down the aisle and give me away. I was bold and took my vows of love to promise hold and cherish all the days of my life to him. He promised the same and instead of taking me on a honey moon we went to my new home in Rhinelander Wisconsin. For the first time in my life I never saw a home so beautiful. It seemed like a dream to me, because all my life all I ever wanted was a great man by my side and I feel like I finally found my soul mate.

The house has 15 bedrooms 10 bathrooms a big dining room, a kitchen that looks like three kitchens and many other sitting rooms. Grape vineyards' along with our own winery, I have a maid and a gardener along with a cook. I am so pleased so far that I hope nothing goes wrong.

We decided to take a honeymoon some other time when we can get someone to watch the children. We wanted to include them in the wedding and festivities. We decided to invite everyone to our new home for the reception. All of the food and family were arriving and Adam showed the children where there new rooms were. Then he said he would show me our room after the children, go to bed and all the guests leave.

We start to have a glass of wine from a winery in

Cape May County called Natalie Woods Vineyards. The vineyards there are incredible. The grapes are so perfect and never out of place on the vines. One of the biggest winery's in South New Jersey. They have incredible choices of wines and incredible variety of Baskets for all occasions. They have their special cheese and crackers and can accommodate any occasion to make the day beautiful, bright, cheerful and festive. They produce all wines from grapes to berries and fruits. Whatever you're tasty, taste buds can handle. Tasting this wine makes me wonder if it is a little dew from heaven.

We also received a great case of Red table Wine from Cape May Winery. One of the biggest winery's in Cape May for just producing grape wines. A very nice man that owns the winery said. Nothing goes through my winery, but grapes. The table wine was bitter sweet, it was heavenly. What wonderful wine for all occasions, this winery produces.

Everyone is real quiet while my father makes a toast. He says may the marriage of Lacey and Adam last a life time. May God Bless them richly.

THE END

www.ingramcontent.com/pod-product-compliance
Ingram Content Group UK Ltd.
Pitfield, Milton Keynes, MK11 3LW, UK
UKHW041933190726
13854UKWH00004B/1555